~ REFLECTIONS ~

By

Theresa Boyd (Lyfe-Poetic)

RoseBud Publishing

© Copyright 2014—Theresa Michelle Boyd
RoseBud Publishing
Staunton, VA 24401
RoseBud_Publishing@yahoo.com

Publisher: RoseBud Publishing
Rights Owner: Theresa Michelle Boyd
Copyright: © 2014 RoseBud Publishing

ISBN 978-0-6924-4236-4

Book design by Theresa M. Boyd
Book editing by Alicia Cole
Cover concept by Theresa M. Boyd
Cover design by Samin Mirgheshmi
Cover image © www.shutterestock.com

Printed in the United States of America

Table of Contents

Expression 1

To Reflect

Silence of My Cry.............................. 3

Ice in the Shades of Light........................... 5

Through the Eyes of Perception................ 7

Articles of Qualms 9

Reflections................................... 11

To Gain Strength

And I Rise 14

Those Days 16

A Disturbed Heart 18

To Release Fustration

Anger..21

Show Me Life 23

To Love

And Then There was Love, So I
Reminisce 26

Seeing Past Your Pain 28

Torn Between Truth and Belief................31

Facilitating in One's Company................. 33

Forever is Timeless...................................... 37

All My Life the Reversal........................... 39

An Invitation to My Love 41

Intimacy Between Lovers and Friends...43

Knowing Love...45

Secret Rain 47

~Expression~

There are so many things that I could say, but first I would like to say thank you to my Lord and Savior Jesus Christ.

Writing has been a passion for many years. This is how I express and reflect, and I am here to share with everyone. In this I hope to connect with all who read my expression... and for those who connect to learn how to reflect with oneself. Expression is who we are and we should not be afraid of expression... and to know... no matter how we feel whether its happiness, sadness, anxiety, depression, faithfulness, loyalty...etc., we all go through life in these different expressions and we all can make it through!

Thank you to all of the people who believed in me and stood by me through all of my expressions - this book is dedicated to you!

With Love,

Lyfe-Poetic

"Creativity is the passion of your reflection." Theresa Boyd

~To Reflect~

Silence of My Cry

Prologue: A morning
of somber voices
and the rain obscures
my cries   I am in a
state of silence
Lord, hear my cry
my life is so hard
it's almost too much
to endure

There are constant
quakes storming in
my heart   and this
day just reminds me
of the destruction of
the paths that seem to
be my future   It's
hard to stay focused
on the good parts that
make up a small
percentage of what is
left of my crossing

All I want is to live
life   with minimal
obstacles, just for a
little while   to know
how it feels to
experience a life
without routine
this is the silence of
my cry

I know I should not
be focused on my past
or my apprehension
of present matters
they should be of no
worry to me   but I
know I can't run or
hide from what my
responsibilities are in
my life

The characteristics of
this world are power
and deceit   to live life
in the pursuit of
happiness.   And in
the design of our
world, this means
only if you can
overcome the rules,

the laws, the money, and the power which seem just out of our reach   And just for those who have

This is the silence of my cry   how can I live if everything around me is based on what you have and what you don't have or the pay you receive based on the skills you may or may not have   and if you have the proper education   how can you live if the barriers are so well blocked that even though you strive to break through, there is always another

barrier   is this our fate?

Does a large part of our world exist in a mass of poverty to keep the small portions of those who are well above their means   in the position of power and greed?

Epilogue: The rain begins to shadow its present routine and the clouds are beginning to accede and there is a small light shining straight from the heavens above   This is the silence of my cry.

Ice in the Shades of Light

Very cold out there
very lonely too.
Where do I find
warmth in this time
of humbleness to be
true? Ice   cool   the
wind is blowing   in
the shades of light
the clouds are misty
not really bright but
not dull either

Mysterious it is
and yet so determined
small clouds began to
form   looking like
solid ice   upon the
ocean surface
beautiful between the
shades of light   the
skies I am referring to

Ideas come from
above   shades of
light, shades of
innocence, shades of
truth, and shades of

purity   not just
during the day   but
all   you can see in
the shades of light

Sundown   the sky
is now somber   not
exactly enlightened
but it has a soft glow.
I would say its mid-
day   when the sun
brightens the skies
again   patches of
blue can be seen
through the ice   in
the shades of light

As time seems to be
immobilized   the
clouds tend to move
on   and the ice
in the shades of light
brightens the day
with its stunning
colors   I see myself
in the delicate shades
in the ice of light
smiling. Humbleness,
happiness, my
enjoyment   of Life.

I'll leave you with
this: Ice   in the
shades of light   is a
warm covering of His
glow,   your warmth
from the cold
Walk beside not
ahead and He shall
guide you through
your life   in the
shade of his light.

Through the Eyes of Perception

In your mind you are right. In my mind you are wrong   we are different   you are a man and I am a woman. But it's not exactly   night and day.

Can't women and men think alike? Or at least value and respect the other's preference   of unspoken words

Perception   is perceived through the philosophy of nature And is released to the receiver   from which the message is the extraction of who's right and who's wrong.   But who's right or wrong? Our own acuity may have

changed the true meaning of what was conveyed

If I relayed an astonishing view then who's to say that perception is not my own, or that there's no diversity in the meaning of what I said? Who's to say that the comprehension of words are shelved or that the significance you took was a word and not it's meaning.

How am I wrong? When the response was not there as quickly as you wished or maybe it was hidden in a secret place between the meaning and the truth. And wasn't it the same many many months ago; now, how can you boldly think so brusquely?

Has it seemed like my thoughts have changed? Is your perception of me so lost that you cannot see the truth in my words? Or is it that you identify your own truth and disregard mine   misleading

yourself and being difficult.

Through the eyes of perception   words can be abstract   or they can be truth

Rely on the truth ask and believe the literal significance for only then will you not be guessing at what's genuine and what's not.

Through the eyes of perception   what's Physical is not always   the truth.

Articles of Qualms

It becomes very interesting when you yearn for the ghastly aspects of your life to go away   it's kind of like asking life to impede the future from happening there are so many chronicles to tell so many decisions to make

Where there are doubts   there are fears   and fears lead to the bleakness of failure. But life goes round right? Is it feasible that half way around life might happen again?

If one's situation illustrates itself back into the formality of the comfort that you created   will it demolish your style of ability   or will it heighten your awareness of delivery

Articles of qualms are anecdotes of one's mentality set forth to prove that life has engrossed itself into meaningless quarrels of seduction   In relation to worries

Without the troubles there could be no qualms   Without the anxiety there could be no fears and without the elevation and depletion of life there is no room to live

The article of qualms
Have multiple sagas
of intensity
waiting among pages
and pages of one's
journal to become
another's legend of
finding the right way
of gaining the
understanding
that life's journeys are

legendary to the life
that one's given to
live.

Articles of qualms are
a part of all life and all
journeys are sacred
all memories are
special and all articles
are true.

Reflections

Long days and short nights   drag along new days and new nights   and she wonders does she really love herself even just a little?

She goes to her mirror and stands before it and in her own reflection she sees nothing   nothing but   deep dark saddening eyes. Her eyes may tell her story

In her own reflection her soul is not in her inner body   but shows on her outer an old soul some would say.

So she takes off her clothes to reveal her nakedness   the nudity that she should not be afraid of   Loving or touching   Her own nakedness. In her reflection she sees a worn out body that went the distance for any and everything she wanted   In her body   her soul that's been hurt or scorned and not by her own indiscretion A soul that tries to reach out   and cannot.

"So what is a person to do?" she thought as she stared into the mirror. She looked at her reflection and smiled   A smile that could learn to love her reflection She touched her arms For their length has gone the journey of her heart

She caressed her stomach   for the hunger has grown and passed   she stroked her legs they are as soft as her eyes   The gentleness of her legs may tell how strongly her successes as well as her defeats

She looked into her mirror at her own reflection   with

passion   a fire that doesn't need to be put out   the desire that lies in the deepest part of her soul, is such love of her own vulnerability She should not be ashamed.

For the new found love of herself   it is her time   my time and no one is going to take that away from me   Reflection Have you genuinely looked at yours?

~To Gain Strength~

And I Rise

One morning I was told to rise and every day I give joy to the light in my life   but still I rise   sadness poured over my soul and still I rise. After a while it felt like no joy was left   and the light had passed and now the love is gone   where did it go?

The passion in my step ceased to exist the courage in my voice appeared as a whisper   The pearl of my eyes seemed to have diminished and I realized I'm not my normal self There is no happiness here   and still I rise.

Days Later   I arose to a gloomy day sarcastic it was for mocking me   I knew I was in bad shape   I was isolating my thoughts and surroundings. Doing more harm than good   but no matter what I did I was truly nowhere around   And so I lay down and I was gone   Lost in thought I was confused and in despair   I was what was I thinking this isn't me?

And I rise   to the sun blinding my sight my thoughts were it has come back to me   my light my joy   I realize that there is someone out here who cares for

me so much   she
casts all her love and
prayers upon me
Through what she
does best   write

I am well   and if
nothing else in the
world could save me
It would be her love
and my faith in who
created me

Now there is the
passion back in my
step   joy within my
smile   light within
my thoughts and
excitement in my
voice   and with
those pearls that I
called my eyes

a diamond appeared
and sparkled to the
lightness of my soul

And the days go by
and the lights are but
a dream   and
when I rise again
I will give all my
thanks for all that I
have and all that I do
not   and if I never
know love again
I know she is the
diamond in my eyes

And so, today I rise.

Those Days

Walking through the sun, passing the rocks of the shore   is he walking with me? The one who carries me when I think I know he's not there?

I've walked a long distance   a journey that ceases to end   troublesome worries when my soul goes down this path but I know he is listening to my expressionless thoughts   not thinking if they may hurt someone else

Those days I was alone   well, I thought   I've came a long way   I desire to come above all those worldly things

that I want because most of all I desire his love; his encouragement; his perfection; his will to forgive and his will to be strong for me

Water softly rolling up and down the shoreline   The sun begins to set   I choose   to sit on the sand to watch the rest of the sunset to enjoy this time without all the worries of my heart. The wind started blowing really hard but I was not cold for more than a second because the warmth of his spirit was near me.

Oh how beautiful I felt   secure in his embrace   So I asked him, "Are you there Lord?" Of course I did not hear his response, but I felt it and that's all I needed   to understand that even when I think he's not listening he is there holding me up to embrace another day

Walking along the shore I awaken to find myself in my own bed   nowhere near water

But how could this be I was just with Him I thanked him for

showing me a vision that in time will come because I need this walk   and this walk will come when I need it the most.

I laid back and smiled soon enough I will have my talk with the one who created me that moment of my life will change me forever

A Disturbed Heart

Walking peacefully
alone   thinking,
thinking, and more
thinking

I was standing in the
middle of the country
road and as the clouds
darkened so did the
sadness in my heart
The rain began to
pour; fast and furious
it was   The
thunder and lightning
became loud and
fierce   there was
nowhere for me to
run or hide

I was drenched; no
need to say head to
toe   but it was so
I was drenched inside
I realized that the
storm was my own
that my heart was
disturbed and that

was why the rain
soaked me so

I could barely see,
walking down the
street   didn't know
where I was going
the wind was
throwing me   from
one way to the other
What was I supposed
to do now?

I fell to my knees and
cried   In the
middle of the road
no one near to help
me find my way
And the rain
continued to pour

At that very moment I
felt a soft hand
embrace my shoulder
and the rain stopped
when I turned to see
He was gone

My heart started to
heal that day and

in spite of everything
it's still healing now

~To Release Frustration ~

Anger

So much pain continuous it seems how I go on   all I feel is rage   and revenge against those who've done me wrong   I feel it with each passing day With every breath I take   I can't understand why I can't let go

                              Anger

Then it brings the past back into right now   and all I see is payback   for my life's troubles, and not the troubles that were caused by me but others

All the tears I shed, all the trials that came to an end and continue to burden me, all the tribulations that began the day I was brought into existence

                              Anger

For all the hard work that feels like failures that are beyond my control

                              Anger

Karma   what did I do to deserve this life I did not ask for   I just want to get away away from all that is troubling my heart The frustrations from my past into the present   I have so much

                              Anger

Upset because happiness does not look like it's in my future

                              Anger

Because I cannot see
beyond what's
happening now

             Anger

Because I can't find
out

             Anger

Because I am not
strong enough to
survive this
tribulation

             Anger

I am angry because
the anger has been
dwelling in the pit of
my being

How do I rid myself
once and for all of
that sin called
Anger? Will someone
show me the way?

Show Me Life

You're in a corner
engaged in a battle
this conflict of life
and death   the
child you carry has no
choice

Your decision will
determine the
outcome of your child
The screams
terminate your
thoughts

And the cries darken
the alley behind you
but yet it was your
choice   it always has
been   to be
promiscuous   no one
to talk to   scared
to confess

Deliberations of what
would be said if
anyone knew
now you're alone

uncertain. Show me
life   give me peace.

Isolated you are
highly disturbed
the gun that eludes
your fingertips
later, re-judging the
aim   you wanted
life   just in that split
second. Now the
blood splatter trickles
down the walls

The pain you wanted
to get away from
you've succeeded
the disappointment
you will suffer   As
the last thought
seeped from your
being

No more life   no
more future   my
black beautiful boy.

Sickness constitutes
the poor   health is
dictated to the rich
the government
institutes what is
disbursed among our
needs   The
president regulates it
all   or does he?
Show me peace
show me heart
show me truth
and determination to
be free outside of
freedom

Show me life and then
there will be peace

Ball your fist up and
watch it in flight
Our world is
shrinking   and
adaptation is scarce
the waters are
polluted   the
ecosystem estranged
our food is rotting
and the people are
scared   who saves
us from extinction

~To Love~

And Then There was Love, So I Reminisce

Is love what comes
from your heart? Or is
it in your soul? Or
maybe it's that
itinerary within the
deepest depths of
your thoughts   on
and on I deliberate
on and on I marvel
so I reminisce

I recall the pain I
endured when the
storm pierced my
world   but don't
let your perceptions
fool you   it's no
tempest of nature
And then there was
love.

Love has many forms
and in the beginning
it was Backstreet's:
Never Gonna Let You Go
he was strong   he
was protective

he was so vivacious
within our
relationship   he was
my first love and he
was my friend   and
so I reminisce

And then there was
love

Isn't it funny how the
impression of love
remains   not
necessarily buried but
just quiet   right
there in the center of
your heart   that's
where it began
Backstreet's: *Never
Gonna Let You Go*
and that is where it
remains   and so I
reminisce

And then there was
love

Love outlines
countless boundaries

and it's up to us to
follow   our
constancy of
emotions   and so
I reminisce   and
do I go on?

Cold winter chills in
the month of red
the roses fall   but
the passion relishes
your name   Your
walk is captivating
it's smooth   it's
sleek   it's willing
it melts my desire
just like

Butta

It's charming   it's
real   it's deep

it's foretold   like a
kinship   our souls
belong   do you not
remember? And shall
I go on? How I
reminisce

And then there was
love

Love is not a game
but it's a choice. Deep
inside   preserved,
the happiness
from which one
learned   That love
is revered
whether it's present
past   or future
It affects who we are.

And then there was
love   so I
reminisce.

Seeing Past Your Pain

Every day I look at
you   I don't look
past you   I don't
look through you
but I look at you
all seems lost   life
seems diminished
where's the sunshine
in the clouds in your
skies? Where is the
love that sought the
rain in your eyes
where is your life?

Life is something you
should enjoy   do
you enjoy your pain?
Why do you hide
behind your pain? I
can help you past
your pain   only if
you let me in, to be in
tune with your pain.
Everything cannot be
left for you to do
alone   and yet I
am here   willing,

wanting   but you
won't let me in.

Am I so horrible of a
person that you dare
not confide in me?
Does it seem like I am
out to hurt you? Do
you not see the tears
that fall from my eyes
every time you turn
me away?

Are you so blind and
confused inside your
own disbelief that
you can't see me at
all? Are you down on
me because of
another?

Another spirit has
hurt you and my
spirit wanders into
the form of them, not
truly being who I am
and all this because
you cannot see past
that hurt or pain

what do you see when
you look at me?

Every day I look at
you   I don't look
past you   I don't
look through you
but I look at you
I look at your warm
state of mind
your happy state of
mind   and then I
look into your deep
dark eyes and see the
pit of your soul
drowning in the
darkness that you
created   and I
sit, wishing you
would let me in to
bring you out

When I look at you
I'm trying to reach
you whether it's with
laughter, or with a
smile and maybe even
a joke or the intimacy
of a touch
something that will
tell me   It's okay to
enter but be careful
with your fragile
heart

Can you see yourself
past your pain? Have
you even thought to
venture outside your
pain? Have you asked
for a shoulder to cry
on   or maybe an
ear to listen? Would
you relinquish all of
you   are you
willing to try?

And   can you
accept someone
loving you past your
pain   with all of

her soul and all of
yours? Just between
you and her   the
tears she feels in her
heart belong to you
can you not feel that
connection?

Can you feel beyond
your soul   let her
hold you until that

moment comes, and
when you awake her
love will still be there
and your pain will
slowly flow away

Every day I look at
you   today
realize that I see you

Torn Between Truth and Belief

How is it difficult to state the truth? What's so essential about being truthful if the other in your life is subject to the feelings that you never correct without bringing great consequences. Why is it so imperative that what I believe is not the belief of the other who comforts me?

I am torn between truth and belief   I know in my heart that the truth needs to be revealed   but shall I hurt the one who I always wanted to have significance in my life?

All these years he never knew how I felt I never said a word because I was not sure of his reaction. I'm so torn between truths which imply that I may fall in love with him again and beliefs that I may never love him the same way   not ever.

Until now I knew I was in love with him so deeply that I could never hurt him no matter how much he hurt me   not until now. I have a belief that the truth hurts and that whoever's truth it is, it's meant to be exposed then he or she will be upset because the world they built is no longer true. The strength of their world can no longer hold on lies.

I believe what was true was that I loved him and continued to wish that he would truly love me. I am torn between truth and belief   I believe he can choose to love me but the truth is he never will   and that hurts so I hurt him by telling him the truth

Why should I remain in pain for his faults and why should I take it upon myself to burden me with all of his faults   no, I can no longer be torn. I have to believe that

he will understand his truth   so he can believe in my truth   so that I can believe in him

Now that I think about it, we need to be true to one another and believe so the future can be promising   I think I will tell him that he is more torn than I, but we can get through it

Torn between truth and belief

Facilitating in One's Company

What is there to hold or give in to one's company? What can you gain or lose? It's human nature to facilitate in the company of someone else's stride   but what if you find yourself not wanting just anyone's stride because you're in one's shadow; a flicker of a judgment that is not true to you or not who you are where do you go?

You say you want to be happy   but what's being happy and do you even know? Are you willing to sacrifice someone else's happiness to receive yours? And if so, what does that say about your character? Are you willing to give yourself completely? Your heart, your soul, your thoughts, your flaws, your body, your mind   to someone else   can you be the company that someone seeks?

Can you honestly not be afraid to become another's without fear   or judgment. To prove to yourself that life is not always about pain and suffering   can you honestly let someone in wholeheartedly and not be troubled by "what-if" and "what could happen"

Can you straightforwardly

give into all your uncertainties and suspicions?

We are all individuals
we are all gifted in
some way or form
it may be clever to say
we are all the same
the way we think, the
way we hear, the way
we solve solutions,
and may be witty to
say that the only
differences between
us are our
experiences   but
that would not make
us individuals
now would it?

Facilitating in one's
company   is
being able to wake up
next to them every
morning

and thank God that
she or he is a part of
your life   and that
He sent a gift   a
person that was made
just for you   no
matter what your
differences are

Facilitating in one's
company   it's like
being free   with
no judgment
they are here to
support you, laugh
with you, joke with
you, cry with you,
share intimate
yearnings with you,
to be there for you
completely   that
person's company
is for you.

That person is here when you are in need, when you need someone to listen, when you are troubled. To hear your sorrows, your joys, your successes, your failures that person is there for you   and you them. Your partner joined together to build a life together and make the most of what life may be left.

There are so many benefits   an abundance if you're open to it

It is so easy when someone knows you so well   that you can look at them and can tell when they are not feeling well, that they have something on their mind, or need to say.

And when you are in that abundance you can, when they feel lonely, or are having problems at work, or just feel a little down when you are in that abundance and are facilitating in one's company you will know without qualm that the person you are joined with is amazingly true and willing   to love and give love purely from their soul.

And when you are untied together at night in your bed you can rest easy because you are true in your heart and she in hers

Can you genuinely look deep within yourself and say you'd rather have multiple persons in your life for each aspect of your life then have that one person to live and live life well with you   to succeed together in a journey in which life is supposed to be free?

Argue that!!!

Forever is Timeless

Endless we are
more like forever
the moments of
truths have always
been   we just never
revealed   the
truth

These nights I've
cried   for the truth
I was told   I may
never forget, but I can
always forgive

Forever is a long time
my love for you is
unconditional
our friendship will
always survive
you are my balance
and I hope I am yours
tonight I cry
because the truth
does hurt, but you are
my balance and I
hope I am yours

forever is a long time
my love is timeless

When days turns into
nights   realize
you've hurt me and I
can't imagine how
much I've hurt you
but endless we are
more like forever
Forgive me for your
pain   it has never
been spoken

I just wish you were
here to balance that
pain   right here by
my side

Face-to-face   will
we rejoin? Is your love
as timeless as mine?
Forever is a long time
                timeless

Will you hold me till
that time?

love is unconditional

don't ever be afraid
I will understand

Unconditional love is
timeless   will you
be my balance and I'll
be yours

Always and forever.

All my Life the Reversal

Every day I spend
without you   my
soul yearns for you
all I want is to spend
the rest of my life
with you

You make me smile
you make me laugh
as well as cry   but
you also give me joy
and happiness. But
you know   when
we fight it destroys
me inside   and
when you don't speak
to me   it hurts my
heart   because I
know I can live
without you but it
will be hard

You please me
you frighten me. But
you also make me
whole   my mind
body. And soul

all I want is to be
with you every day of
my life for the rest of
my life

I'm so in love with
you   it burns my
heart inside   and
when it rains   I

wonder where you
are and why you are
not here beside me
I think of how you
feel and how you're
doing   would you
ever tell me?

What I really want to
know is   what
completes you   do
I?

I want to know how
you're hurting and
what hurts you most
I want to know what

frightens you and
what you are afraid of
the most.

I want to know what
makes you happy
and what gives you
happiness. I want to
know what makes
you sad and what
gives you sadness. I
want to know what

drives you and
sometimes make you
distant

But most of all I want
to know   do you
love me enough to
want to spend every
day of your life for the
rest of your life with
me

I love you.

An Invitation to My Love

How many times have
you wanted love?
True
unconditional
pure love. Have you
ever questioned when
it will arrive? And
will you ever know
it's there?

Here I am   waiting
wanting   your
unconditional love
as the breeze
embraces my soul. I've
invited you   and
yet you're still not
here

Maybe my love is not
what you need   or
want. Maybe it's
someone else's love
you fathom
maybe I thought
I saw love in your
eyes or maybe it was

lust   you had for
me as we made love.

I've given you an
invitation to my love
to explore the
pureness in my soul
the unconditional
beat in my heart
the truths of my body
I gave   you
me and all I had
and maybe that's not
enough,

Love lasts forever
pure   unconditional
and true   it will
never change
but my love for you is
hanging with each
passing day. And as
your soul searches for
the truth in the love
you need   you
will be passing me
without notice

between the sunrises.
When the next two
moons appear you'll
be waiting for me
but I'll be gone.

My invitation to you
cannot last forever
for I will need to find
a love of my own
and if I never find it
I'll know that once I
gave all my love for
one who could not
love me back

An invitation for my
love   as true
as unconditional
and as pure   as
love can be   blink
twice when enough is
enough and I will be
gone.

This invitation has
been sent!

Intimacy Between Lovers and Friends

The way I see you
is the way I will want
to see the man of my
dreams   the
steadiness in your
voice frightens me
and soothes me all in
the same notion of
time. Having the best
of both worlds
is like making love to
your mind   lovers
and friends.

To have an intimacy
that no one else can
share because their
mind does not
comprehend the
reality, or the unique
connection, that one
must go through to
have that special
relationship

Intimacy   is a rare
occasion that one

shares with another
the way your voice
lingers through every
vessel in my body
that's intimacy
how every time we
talk   the language
of your speech
that's intimacy
being lovers and
friends
confidants and
companions
means everything to
me   that's
intimacy   the way
I see it.

Just think about it
we already made
romantic journeys
with one another
just not physically.
And my
understanding of your
demeanor will never
change   you are a

man   my friend
my inspiration
my hero   and to
have all that in one
person is a lifetime of
treasures that I will
bury deep inside
and only you will find
it   when you're
ready to receive it.

Lovers   happen
when we hold no
boundaries in that
moment   where
it's just you and I
no one can change it
or sugarcoat it
it's like a dream
you manifest your
desires
eventually you will
make them come true.

Friends   we can
hold intimate
discussions
where we know the
other is not judging
our every word

we can talk into the
twilight of the night
without interruption
we can allocate our
deepest secrets and
know that it will not
seep out amongst
the mouths that tell
all   we are
friends above all else.
And nothing could
destroy that intimacy
of being friends.

Being lovers and
friends   is like
being intimate with
your soul   it's all
in the mind   and
if you can adapt
to that then the
pleasures are yours.
Lovers and friends
there's nothing more
worth keeping
but the intimacy of
being who we are

      Lovers and Friends.

Knowing Love

There are three phases regarding the nature of love: having loved being loved and the knowledge of love it's nothing like knowing the truth about love it's like tasting love for the first time.

Love has heart love has passion love has soul. Love knows tears. Love knows deception love knows anger love knows desire love knows the truth and most of all love knows fear.

Phase One: Having loved most people desire the love of truth and serenity of others' loyalties to collapse in another's arms having the passion to look into one's eyes and tell the truth of the feelings that swept you away. Inside the nature of love the beauty of knowing you are capable of having love to join the company of being loved.

Phase Two: Being loved is like watching the rain cover your soul with a blanket of trust knowing that you are loved is like singing to the sound of wind chimes blowing from one side to the other in the fragrance of

your heart. For the
one receiving the love
the aspects of truth
reside in one's
knowledge of love.

Phase Three:
Knowledge of love
is like a fear of
purifying one's spirit
first the anger
then the tears
and a mountain of
deception   but
knowing all that
comes with the
knowledge of love
holds the truth
of all fears   all
trust   all desires
all deception   all
of your heart
and soul   all of
your affection
rounded up in one
small piece of
tranquility   for
you to manage the

knowledge of love
is like staring at an
ocean's spring
and turning from hot
to cold   in the
mysterious form of
division.

The three phases
what do they mean
well   when the air
becomes too crisp and
coldness starts to
settle in   and his
arms become heat on
your existing body
you will know what
they mean   and
that is

Opportunity
peace   and
enjoyment.

Knowing love   is
the key to the
existence of your
heart.

Secret Rain

It's so oblivious not
really ridiculous
but strange and
mysterious   I'm
relating to my rain
ridiculed in self-
defense   it's a
secret   not
totally dismissed but
it's true I must admit
this rain sees an end
where do I begin?

Secrets lie beneath
the scorching sun
the rain cools off the
spirit's drum
hold off a moment let
me lie below these
skies and tell the
truth in his midst
before you see my
dust at its end. One
moment let me breath
I can't believe it's
raining again

It's a place where no
one has entered
scared to deliver
love is so strong
there's no willing
participant   it's
so unfortunate
beautifully sculpted
lies in its own format,
my secret rain

Between, the rain
bears a sound   lost
and long   so soft
so delicate   so far
it's hard
forbidden to touch,
it's a wonder how I
carried it this much.
It's pouring now
along the ridges the
water falls   in the
abyss I fall   the
mountain in its cause
how powerful in its
own form   what
does it all mean. A

secret rain   secret
fall   the truth
repels us all.

The rain has slowed
but for how long
my spirit expires with
a drop of a rose. In the
beginning I was lost
in the end I began
full circle it reigns so
where do I
commence? My rain is
where I live   it's
where I began
but there's no telling
how it will end

And in awe it's
beautifully sculpted
oh it lies in its own
deliverance   and
it's drowning in its
own remembrance
and waiting to be
liberated but that's
just my secret

rain

~ REFLECTIONS ~

www.ingramcontent.com/pod-product-compliance
Lightning Source LLC
LaVergne TN
LVHW010023070426
835508LV00001B/21